AF424305

SUFFER LESS

Other books by
BLACK AUSAR

Soul Searching Poetry

Crowns and Shattered Dreams

MEDITATIONS FOR TRANSFORMING TRAUMA INTO HEALING

SUFFER LESS

BOOK KING PUBLISHING, INC.
DENVER, COLORADO

Copyright © 2023 Jason L. Shankle

Published by Book King Publishing, Inc.
Editorial and Production: Jason L. Shankle
Cover Illustration Painter: @Ravensart333
Cover Graphic Designer: @AngelicaShankle.Art
Typology: Jason L. Shankle

All rights reserved. This book may not be used or reproduced in whole or in part without the written permission from the author/publisher, except in the case of brief quotations embodied in critical articles or reviewer who may quote brief passages in a review; nor may any part of this book be reproduced, stored in a retrieval system, or transmitted in any form or by any means – electronic, mechanical, photocopying, recording, or other, including information storage systems, without written permission from the author/publisher.

ISBN: 979-8-218-21440-1
Printed in the U.S.
10 9 8 7 6 5 4 3 2 1

To the Highest Supreme Source for guiding
and protecting me along my divine walk.
To my ancestors, children and my wisdom team
that keep me spiritually balanced.

CONTENTS

A Note from the Author...8

1
<u>From Suffering to Understanding</u>
The Observational Eye.....11
Embracing the Hurt...76

2
<u>The Road to Self-Compassion</u>
Time and Your Heart...133
Finding Inner Peace...155

3
<u>Dismantling Toxic Trauma Cycles</u>
Recycling Energetic Emotions...201
Breaking Family Generational Curses...228

4
<u>The Essence of Healing</u>
Post-Traumatic Growth...254
Burning Questions/Writing Prompts
for Deeper Healing...280

About the Author...303

This book, "*Suffer Less*" was written to create this understanding of ones self through meditative quotes, with writing prompts at the end. These meditations are designed to be digested in your subconscious by being still to have awareness of who you are. To say you will never suffer is illogical but to suffer less is possible. Our perception are indicators of our behavior and spiritual identity. Adapting to the now is more important than your past because that is done and the future is not here yet. Self-compassion is at the heart of understanding your authentic true self in order to experience inner peace.

    Meditations for Transforming Trauma into Healing, will influence you to sit with your philosophies and reasoning mind. One line can make you feel like you read an enitre book. They are meditations aimed for you to intentionally pause or say that's interesting I've never thought about that... *Suffer Less* has tested me throughout life with this book being a supreme enlightenment for myself to write these meditations. My hope is that you receive a healing message to remind you to suffer less and know you have greatness inside of you.

Dedicated to The Most High Supreme Source

SUFFER LESS
Meditations for Transforming Trauma into Healing

FROM SUFFERING TO UNDERSTANDING
THE OBSERVATIONAL EYE

A healthy person to me is someone who adapts to
every circumstance in any weather even when it
rains on them.
They embrace the shower cleanse and feel God's
tears drenching them
while saying thank you for this experience.

You don't know what
you would never say
in the future
or what circumstances
would influence you to do
what you haven't done, yet
remember this before
you say "never."

You create the life
you make.

If you give someone knowledge
it will last longer than giving them money.

Nothing more, nothing less, hope for the best.

People can't help who they are…
Let them be.

It is only the wise that sits in the storm wondering
how to water the seeds that aren't
in the ground.

Soulful creativity is looking into the window
of the spirit while being tapped in
with intent.

If you don't like everything you eat;
You sure won't like everyone you meet.

Money is based in philosophies that demands
the maintenance of emotional attachments to people
to materials.

Don't let expectations kill the moment.

Treat change like change and every meaningful
moment as a hundred-dollar bill.

If you don't know your history others will write it
and your lack of discernment will make you believe
everything you hear without understanding and
nothing you see.

You create our own feelings.

The constant "ifs" create
mental confusion and delusions.

Healing is contagious.

It's not if uncertain things will happen it is when.

Worry not about tomorrow because it hasn't got
here yet.

Take advantage of your disadvantages.

You don't have to look for trouble;
Trouble has your address.

Change the way you solve problems,
So, you are not captive by your expectations and
others.

Life is short but long with perspective.

Being adaptive is one of the best medicines.

What others eat doesn't make your stomach hurt.

It doesn't only take diligence to make great decisions; but self-restraint to be patient.

Sometimes the best decision is to make no decision.

You can't miss a dish that you haven't tasted.

There is always time to practice patience's somewhere.

Trying to control others perception is like wrestling
a tornado down to the ground.

The journey only appears long because of your
perception not your view.

In order to be woke both eyes must be open not
blind in one while blurry in the other.

Don't let people give you luggage that is not yours.

The things we tolerate is what makes life; not things
we cannot change.

Money is the worst thing that could have happened
to some people.

Pain makes you learn just as experience makes you wise.

When you operate in the false self you become the
first liar you see.

Tell one lie you have to tell another.
with the truth you only have to tell it once.

If you live in truth your actions will follow.

Struggles is a part of progress like experiences is
needed to be better.

Wants are like wishes; whenever you make one you
desire another.

When you find the lesson, you will learn how to understand.

What you think people think of you is just an
opinion and nothing more.

The only way to get over complacency is to be uncomfortable.

When you think you've seen it all; you will see
something new.

The "Now" doesn't wait on the past or chase the future.

The universe knows what you need before you do.

Don't let your next decision be a regretful lesson.

We are not who we use to be.

Be careful what you believe.

There are many ways to fix a problem but it's better
to heal.

It is impossible to live an enjoyable life without
taking risks.

To prove your happiness to others is when you
decide to settle for subconscious misery.

Even a wealthy person without happiness is a poor
person.

The quicker you can look fear in the eyes,
the sooner you can stare at your healed reflection.

Without some mistakes there would be no answers.

Never take freedom for granted.

Don't allow fear to chain you to a toxic narrative.

Your destiny is one of the most expensive things
you will ever pay for.
You must believe you can heal before starting this
journey to autonomy.

The world stops for no one.

Its only too late when you die.

If you don't choose yourself; no one else can either.

You must find yourself first before you can find
someone else.

Don't allow the past to steal your present.

Silent confidence is the loudest thing in the room.

Taking care of your time is taking care of your
heart.

<u>EMBRACING THE HURT</u>
You are more than the experiences of what
happened to you.

Stop giving people the benefit of doubt
when you should be doubting the benefits.

Being a healer is painful
and to say to the universe
"I want to be wise"
means you are asking
for light and dark life experiences
in order to know the difference.

A piece of peace will only leave
fragments of autonomy.

Your expectations must leave room
for mistakes and conflict if you want to
be free.

The only way to change it is to understand it.

It is impossible to go throughout life without loss
so be mindful of how you live.

Be honest… Don't choose to lie about your
suffering.

If you are passive, you will never get things done
even when you die people will say you enjoyed it
because you never spoke up. Speak up!

It's either you pay, or you pay.

The quicker you let it go the faster you can grow.

Don't be a slave to your own rules and emotions.

Once you spend your time you can't get it back:
Like the past.

Don't be a slave to your own rules and emotions.

Once you spend your time you can't get it back:
Like the past.

Everyone needs help… Even you need help…

Peace isn't that far.

It's not compromising when you choose to suffer in silence because of your attachments to the false self.

The real challenge is to be comforted
with the things that are immeasurable.

You must be selfish with your depression than focus
on soothing your suffering.

The Universe will challenge you to see how much
you want to heal.

Your destiny is the most expensive thing you will
ever pay for.

Worry not about the future because it doesn't exist
yet.
Living happy is only difficult if you are faking it
but if you are happy,
you would just be in the now.

If you are in fear of pain, you will be terrified of growth.

Don't be mad at experience because without it we
know nothing.

The thing you run from will one day sit with you.

Struggle and purpose require the same amount of
energy. The choice is yours…

Whatever you are going through you can get
through.

Sometimes you have to take the chip on your
shoulder; dip then eat it.

Life will always be an uphill battle with an
unbalanced heart and mind.

Use fear like fuel to get to the finish line.

Pain is something we need to remember and learn
lessons.

Every bite of the fruit may not be sweet as some
good advice could taste bitter.

Healing is designed to sometimes be painful to
change your perception,
so, it does not handcuff you to fear.

Don't allow your past story to be the reason you
lack compassion for yourself and future.

If you can't learn from losing you will be surprised
when you win.

Temporary setbacks make for a great comeback.
You will thrive.

Experience doesn't care about how you feel.

Fear is like an induced cancer only you can cure
with your mind.

Embrace the challenge because it may be an
opportunity.

Problems are defined by your perception.

Sometimes you don't know what you need until you
are starving.

Don't let depression make your decisions.

Some pains are only met to be leased not owned.

If you don't know how to use the tools,
they will only take up space.

The mind is a terrible thing to waste; so is your
spirit.

Don't allow fear to be the creative director of your dreams.

You must help yourself before helping others.

Don't be chained to a narrative that doesn't exist.

Sometimes when you have done your best you must
leave regret behind.

There is no perfect direction because life is full of
beautiful mistakes.

You must remember that you are not the only one
experiencing what you are feeling.

Pain can be a kind teacher if you let it.

Critical self-talk is the main ingredient in guilt.

Some tests are meant to define you… not punish
you.

128

Fear is what cages the mind; healing is what frees
the spirit.

Maybe your suffering is too much right now
because there is still healing that needs to be done.

Don't allow fear to hijack your growth.

When you run from yourself; you will only run into
your "self".

THE ROAD TO SELF-COMPASSION
<u>TIME AND YOUR HEART</u>

Wherever you find your time, you find your heart.
Don't waste your heart.

If you don't choose yourself; no one else can either.

If you don't manage your heart right,
You will always be broke.

Never compromise of your value.

Time, Self-Love, Acceptance and Forgiveness are
the most valuable things you can give yourself.

When you value yourself you save your own time.

When you are valuing your emotional equity you
can afford more help.

There are some happy moments you should treat
like forever.

As soon as you can release the past.
the closer you are to being healed.

You teach people how to treat you so don't mistreat
yourself.

You don't have to check the tag when you know
your worth.

You can't please everyone and even if you could;
you cannot do it at the same time.

If your happiness is based upon someone else's
perception, you will forever fall short.

Never put your relationship higher than the priority
of self-love. One way to get to the next phase in life
is to take a leap for better.

If you fight acceptance of the true self, you will lose
every time.

The most difficult person to forgive and trust is
yourself.

Don't exhaust yourself by not being yourself.

Don't live to die while dying to live.

Put yourself in the position to invest in yourself.

Make today count towards your destiny.

Don't be scared to choose yourself.

You are stronger than you think you are.

FINDING INNER PEACE

There is not a more difficult enemy than the ego nor
is there a greater victory once you conquer
the ugly parts of your "self".

Everything is intertwined somehow in this journey
we call life so never forget who you are
in your story.

To succeed you must believe in
your "self" even when things
seem impossible because through
pain you grow.

Self-acceptance is contingent upon how you treat
yourself.
And less about how others feel and think about you.

Everyone life's experience is customize to their
existence.

Meditations are for understanding yourself.

You are not even the same. I wasn't born an author
yet; I am an author. I wasn't born a therapist;
yet I became a therapist.
And I was and is innocent in my own right;
yet I will die according to how I see myself.

Be your own mental assistant.

162

Patience is a skill not an attribute.

The secret weapon for self-hate is compassion.

Being impartial to your thoughts and not persuaded
by them helps you be more creative with your
healing and patient with your trauma triggers.

Attachments are the enemy to self-improvement.

The closet you will get to perfection is
imperfection.

If you could only appreciate what you don't know
as much as you do know…
There will always be hope to be a better version of
yourself.

Use more than what your eyes see because your
view is only perception.

You can never run from yourself because eventually
your conscience will catch you.

Don't allow anyone to break your spirit not even
yourself.

Don't be a slave to prescribed opinions.

Be who you are and stop worrying about what
people think of you.

Don't handover yourself to thoughts that have
nothing to do with you.

Identify when your expectations are ruling your
emotions.

Speak your truth and don't fall for lies.

What is for you is looking for you as well.

Sometimes the answer is in the question.

You can't fake authenticity.

Being who you are should not take away from what
you are about.

Don't ever let anyone break your spirit. ANYONE!

Some journeys can't have passengers.

Heal your spirit because you owe it to yourself.

Believe in yourself because you are the first person
to encounter your dreams.

Sometimes what you are searching for is inside of
you!

Don't be a slave to your false narrative.

You are the common denominator… You choose
the formula.

Don't allow the past to steal your present.

Self-love is the first love.

No one has a story like yours! No one.

It is impossible to be perfect so embrace your flaws.

Sometimes the answer is acceptance.

Self-care is a powerful weapon… use it!

Balance is a symptom of harmony.

Unconditional acceptance is one of the best gifts
you can ever give yourself.

Follow your intuition; your spirit will thank you later!

Be sure to be conscious of what health vs critical
self-talk does to your emotions.

The most difficult expectations to accomplish are
the ones we place on ourselves.

Don't allow fear to blind your vision.

Without acceptance there is no self-love.

DISMANTLING TOXIC TRAUMA CYCLES
<u>RECYCLING ENERGETIC EMOTIONS</u>

War is forever
you can only
maintenance the battles.

Fear is an amazing phenomenon.

There is power in admitting.

The thing about "brush it off" is it piles up under
the mat in the middle of the room.

You can't pass off your shadow.

Just because I am letting you go doesn't mean I am
giving up on you.

Never risk your life for someone who doesn't care
about yours.

The thing about mistakes is that
you can't take them back.

Just because you are not hitting the person doesn't
mean you can't beat them with your words.

When you are taught to be ill don't be surprised
when you behave in a sick manner.

It shouldn't take dying in order for you to
pay attention to your health.

What you feed you mind consumes your heart.

Acceptance is not just a choice but a committed
decision of your will.

You can help people get things; but it is up to them
to determine what things become.

You are than the experience of what happened.

Circumstances happens to you don't let it become
you.

The past is a ghost that only comes alive because of
your energy.

Denial never helped anything grow.

Silence is a loud teacher for the ignorant.

Perfect is impossible.

Being successful is addictive,
Don't become an addict.

If drama is your spiritual food, you are in trouble.

Be aware of your vices because
it has numerous flavors.

Misunderstanding and disrespect can sometimes
look like twins.

The all-or-nothing philosophy actually
takes your options away.

Pride comes with shame that turns into
self-resentment.

Only nobodies hate on somebodies.

BREAKING FAMILY GENERATIONAL CURSES

A person can never use not having a father/mother as an excuse to not be a dad/mom because even though he/she wasn't there. Do the opposite of what was done to you because you know how it is to be that neglected child.

Breaking the chains of trauma births post-traumatic growth.

Recycle your knowledge and protect your seeds.

One can act like they are listening,
but one cannot fake caring.

Trauma is like a shadow everywhere you go
It goes with you.

Just because you talk or see someone everyday
doesn't mean you know what they are going
through.

The same sword you swing around carelessly will
cut you one day.

Fame is one of the most addictive drugs that can
either heal or destroy legacies.

If there is no healing it's not healed.

Don't turn over a new leaf; uproot the toxic trunk of
this old tree.

Don't get over it; get through it.

Trauma is not a death sentence, just a line in your
story.

Cycles end when you stop running and confront the
real issues.

Trauma and pain can hide the questions and
answers to your healing.

Don't underestimate your trauma. Get healed!

Break generational curses by addressing your
family trauma.

Be the break in your family generational trauma
chain.

You must discover the cycle before you can stop it.

Starve the family secrets that feed generational curses.

Break the trauma loop with truth and awareness.

Generational curses are breaking as you read.
Our tribes are like forests that must be protected.

Un-respectful people are so hard to respect.

Don't allow your pride to keep you hungry.

Watch what you start because it may finish you.

You are bias to your own views.

Toxic pride will destroy you from the inside out.

THE ESSENCE OF HEALING
POST-TRAUMATIC GROWTH

If you are mad at me, tell no one else but me…

You can't convince a fool to have common sense.

To be someone you are not
is to be a willing prisoner.

Aim for your passion and land on your purpose.

When you rush you miss windows of
opportunities as well as doors to alternative
destinies.

There is power in understanding!

The healing language is spoken through the work.

Some journeys can't have passengers.

The difference between a wise and a foolish person
are their decisions and ability to learn from their
experiences.

At some point we will all experience the losses of
Death, ex's, emotions, feelings, love and self.

Creativity is a symptom of healing and wellness.

Sometimes healing has to bother you in an
uncomfortable good way.

You are a warrior and no matter the terrain
you will conquer it.

Once you meet a level of acceptance you won't be
impacted by your circumstances.

Your pain may not be for you.
It may be for you to help someone else heal.

Sometimes it only takes your presence to support others.

The irony in healing is when you feel pain you
know you are doing it right.

Healing is a process not a conquest.

Healing can feel like pain because you are touching
something you ignored.

With God being inside of us that makes us Gods;
and the Universe is our Source connection to all
healing, love, compassion, vulnerability,
and understanding to overcome all timeline hexes,
family generational trauma and curses in any
dimension, realm, energy exchange, before and
after the womb.

Please do free association writing to the following prompts in your journal, and/or take out a piece of paper. And answer these questions.

BURNING QUESTIONS AND WRITING PROMPTS FOR DEEPER HEALING

Just because you don't like that person,
Doesn't mean you can't respect them.
Haven't you respected people you don't like or even
known before?

If you asked for it and God gave it to you,
Then why didn't you expect it?

Why do you believe you are
supposed to have things you want?

Does the result of what you see in your vision
pleasing to you?

Who do you blame when you slip on ice?
Do you blame the universe, the ice, mother nature,
God, or yourself?
When you can see what blame actually is;
you will find the answer in your reasoning.

If you have to call a plumber to fix your pipes;
And contact an electrician to power your electricity;
A roofer to repair a leak in your roof;
Why wouldn't consult with a therapist for your
mental health?

When are you going to choose yourself?

What will it take to change your spiritual diet?

If time heals all wounds so does acceptance?
What do you believe?

If you use the same formula that produces failure,
why would you expect different results?

Are the systems you live by peaceful in your mind?

Have confidence in your ability to speak with
conviction and execute with surety.
Are you your true self in your relationships?

Money are seeds. What are you growing?

You can love anything; but can you understand?

Do you see the chink in your own armor protecting
you?

If it weren't for the tests of life, would you know
your strengths?

You attract who you are. What do you see?

How is your spirit feeling today?

If only positivity was more preferred over
negativity.
How balanced could you be?

Wisdom requires curiosity and understanding not
just seeking.
What are you seeking?

Don't allow trauma to be a script writer for your
life. What are you writing about your story?

-"He/She has an anger problem"
Or
"He/She has a hurt problem"
Can you hear the difference when said out loud?

What will you see in your final movie... The end of
the world is the day you die. If you were at your
funeral what would you say at your eulogy?

ABOUT THE AUTHOR

I am a Father, Healer, Therapist, Author, Poet, Self-Proclaim Black Consciousness Historian, and Philosopher. My professional identity as a therapist and owner of my private therapy practice Inner Self and Wisdom, LLC has been a significant part of my healer's aura. To walk in my purpose of helping individuals, couples, families, and the Black Communities mental health is one of the greatest honors I'm blessed to experience. I am the only author and owner of Book King Publishing, Inc. I am the author of *Soul Searching Poetry, Crowns and Shattered Dreams* and *Suffer Less: Meditations for Transforming Trauma into Healing*. Lastly, I share my wisdom on my social media outlets and YouTube Channel "A Moment with Jason Shankle".